**gage**

# Canadian Beginner's DICTIONARY

Senior Consultant
Ron Benson

© 2002 Gage Learning Corporation
164 Commander Blvd., Toronto, ON M1S 3C7

All rights reserved. No part of this work covered by the copyrights hereon may be reproduced or used in any form or by any means—graphic, electronic, electrostatic, or mechanical—without the prior written permission of the publisher or, in case of photocopying or other reprographic copying, a licence from the Canadian Copyright Licensing Agency.

Any request for photocopying, recording, taping, or information storage and retrieval systems of any part of this book shall be directed in writing to the Canadian Copyright Licensing Agency, One Yonge Street, Suite 1900, Toronto, Ontario, M5E 1E5.

Original text and design: The Macquarie Library Pty Ltd ©1998

We acknowledge the financial support of the Government of Canada through the Book Publishing Industry Development Program for our publishing activities.

We acknowledge the Government of Ontario through the Ontario Media Development Corporation's Ontario Book Initiative.

**We wish to thank the following educators for their advice and assistance:
Stephen Dow and Kathryn Mattison**

**National Library of Canada Cataloguing in Publication Data**
Main entry under title: The Gage Canadian beginner's dictionary
(Gage Canadian reference series)

ISBN 0-7715-2011-5
1. English language—Dictionaries, Juvenile. I. Title. II. Series.
PE1628.5.G323 2002      j423      C2002-900604-X

Illustrations: Beth Norling
Design and additional illustrations: ArtPlus Limited

ISBN **0-7715-2011-5**
2 3 4 5 FP 06 05 04 03
Written, printed, and bound in Canada

---

### GAGE CANADIAN REFERENCE SERIES

**Gage Canadian Dictionary**
**Gage Canadian Thesaurus**
**Gage Canadian Concise Dictionary**
**Gage Canadian Writer's Handbook**

**Gage Canadian Intermediate Dictionary**
**Gage Canadian Student Writer's Guide**

**Gage Canadian Junior Dictionary**
**Gage Canadian School Dictionary**
**Gage Canadian School Thesaurus**
**Gage Canadian Writers in Action Handbook**

**Gage Canadian Beginner's Dictionary**
**Gage Canadian First Book of Words**

# Contents

Dictionary Skills Begin Here . . . . . . . . . . . . 4

Using the Dictionary . . . . . . . . . . . . . . . . . 5

Dictionary Activities . . . . . . . . . . . . . . . . . 6

Gage Canadian Beginner's Dictionary . . . 12

Appendix . . . . . . . . . . . . . . . . . . . . . . . . 118
   Words We Use a Lot . . . . . . . . . . . . . . 118
   Colours . . . . . . . . . . . . . . . . . . . . . . . 122
   Numbers . . . . . . . . . . . . . . . . . . . . . . 123
   Coins . . . . . . . . . . . . . . . . . . . . . . . . 123
   Shapes . . . . . . . . . . . . . . . . . . . . . . . 124
   Solids . . . . . . . . . . . . . . . . . . . . . . . . 125
   Days . . . . . . . . . . . . . . . . . . . . . . . . 126
   Months . . . . . . . . . . . . . . . . . . . . . . 126
   Seasons . . . . . . . . . . . . . . . . . . . . . . 126
   Our Solar System . . . . . . . . . . . . . . . 127
   Map of Canada . . . . . . . . . . . . . . . . 128

# Dictionary Skills Begin Here

The *Gage Canadian Beginner's Dictionary* has three primary uses:

### ➤ as a source of word meanings

The picture and accompanying sentence combine to provide a word definition. The picture of an ambulance gives the reader a lot of information. However, it's when that information is combined with the information in the sentence that the child will understand that an ambulance is a vehicle for going to a hospital.

**ambulance**
An ambulance takes people to a hospital.

### ➤ as a provider of correct word usage

Words are used in the context of full sentences to demonstrate their correct usage.

**down**
Diane is going down the slide.

### ➤ as a resource for conventional spelling

In the beginning stages of writing, children create their own word spellings by combining their knowledge of sound-symbol correspondence (phonics), their visual memory (how they "see" the word in their mind), and how they hear the word (auditory perception). These temporary spellings eventually give way to the question, "How do you spell . . . ?" The *Gage Canadian Beginner's Dictionary* provides children with the conventional spelling of a storehouse of those most-requested words.

The words that are found in the *Gage Canadian Beginner's Dictionary* have many sources, including the *Gage Canadian Spelling* Series and the *Reading Teacher's Book of Lists*. You will find:

- the first 300 most common words in the English language. These words make up about 65 percent of all written material.

- the majority of the 1000 most common words

- less common words that are useful to young children

- a collection of theme words: days of the week, shapes, colours, and so on.

In total, there are more than 1200 words for children to look at, to talk about, to "play with," to build into their spoken and written vocabularies, to learn to read, and to enjoy.

# Using the Dictionary

This section is for those teachers, parents, or other adults who will be using the *Gage Canadian Beginner's Dictionary* with a child or group of children, in a school or home setting.

Many of the activities on the following pages can be used in situations with one child, with a pair or small group of children, or with a large group. For easier reading, we have used the word *children* to mean an individual child, a small group of children, or a class of children.

## A Walk Through

To introduce the *Gage Canadian Beginner's Dictionary* and to help the children identify ways in which a reference book is organized, you could take the children on a walk through the book. Invite them to look at the various features listed below, and to talk about what they see.

### The cover

**Ask:** Why do books have titles? Why are there pictures on the cover?

### The large letters at the top of the page

**Ask:** What do the large letters at the top of each page tell you?

### The alphabet across the top of the page

**Ask:** How does the alphabet across the top of each page help you?

### The words in boldface

**Ask:** Why are these words bigger than the others?

### The visuals (photographs and sketches)

**Ask:** How do the pictures help you to read the words?

### The sentences below the visuals

**Ask:** Can you tell something else about the big word? or Can you answer the question?

### The Appendix of word lists and theme words

**Ask:** Have you seen this word before? Can you use this word to tell something?

> Knowing the names of the alphabet letters and the position of each in the alphabet is important to the effective use of the dictionary. You and the children should sing the alphabet song often while pointing to the letters across the top of any page.

To get the children talking about the dictionary and to sustain their interest in it, they could be invited to look for familiar words and for interesting pictures, and then to report back on their findings.

# Dictionary Activities

The following is a selection of activities to introduce and reinforce various dictionary skills, such as recognizing the various alphabet letters and securing their position. The activities are grouped according to the nature of their word focus, rather than in order from easier to more difficult. You will be able to select those tasks that best suit the abilities, skills, and current learning needs of the particular child or group of children you're working with.

## Spot the Letter

To help the children become more familiar and secure with the position of the alphabet letters, have them identify the location of various letters as *near the beginning*, *in the middle*, or *near the end*. Invite them to look at the alphabet printed across the top of the Aa pages and ask:

Where is the letter D — near the beginning, in the middle, or near the end? Beginning, middle, or end — J?

To reinforce the letters, print them on chart paper or the chalkboard as you say their names. Be sure to position the letters correctly in relation to their alphabetical order.

As a variation, you could divide the children into three groups: Beginning (letters A to F), Middle (G to Q), and End (R to Z). Call out a letter, and have the children stand (or raise their hands, or repeat the letter after you) if the letter "belongs to" their group.

To refine the positional language as *before*, *after*, *following*, *first*, *second*, *twelfth*, and so on, ask:

What letter comes before C? After M? What letter follows X? What is the eighth letter in the alphabet? Does G come before or after H? Does O come before or after N? Does G come before or after B? Does R come before or after Y?

Have the children confirm the positions by finding a B page, an L page, and so on.

## A Letter Race

To secure the children's knowledge of the position of the alphabet letters, invite one child to call out a letter and have the others find that page in their dictionary, or on the alphabet chart.

## Sing the Alphabet Song

Sing the alphabet song together as you point to a posted alphabet chart. To give the children practice finding various letter pages, sing the alphabet song to them and stop at various letters at which time they can search for and locate a page that corresponds to the letter you stopped at.

To help anchor the letter's location, always start singing from the beginning of the alphabet — the children will hear that, for example, *C* is near the beginning, *M* is near the middle, and *Y* is near the end.

## Point to the Letter

To secure the recognition of the various alphabet letters, point to a letter on an alphabet chart or on alphabet cards. Have the children point to the same letter in the alphabet across the top of any page of the *Gage Canadian Beginner's Dictionary*. Invite a volunteer to name the letter.

## I'm Thinking of a Letter

Play a game that focusses the children on the position of the letters in the alphabet, identifies something about the shape of the letter, and offers an example of a word that begins with the letter. Say:

I'm thinking of a letter that is
- near the beginning of the alphabet
- made of four straight lines
- the first letter in the word *exit*

or
- near the middle of the alphabet
- the shape of a circle
- the first letter in the word *open*

To emphasize the location of the letter in the alphabet (very useful knowledge that makes using a dictionary more efficient), you could say the three clues, then repeat the first one.

## Add an Ending

Invite the children to use words from the dictionary to help you make new words using the most common suffixes *-s, -ing, -ed, -er, -est, -ly*. Suggest or elicit, for example, gift/gifts, go/going, jump/jumped, fast/faster, fast/fastest, glad/gladly.

## Rhyme Time

To reinforce rhyming words, have the children open the dictionary to a particular page. For example, you might choose page 46.

**Ask:** Can you put your finger on a word or picture that rhymes with *name*? **(game)** *late*? **(gate)** *pet*? **(get)**

Check to be sure that the children have found the correct word/picture.

This game can be extended:

**Ask:** Can you think of a word that rhymes with *game*? *gate*?

and so on, using words from the chosen page.

When the children become familiarized and comfortable with the routine — and sufficiently skilled — invite them to create and ask the questions.

## Sames and Opposites

To introduce and reinforce synonyms and antonyms, have the children turn to a particular page. For example, you might choose page 62.

**Ask:** Can you find a word that means the same as *grass*? **(lawn)**
Can you find a word that means the opposite of *right*? **(left)**

## Printing Letters

To encourage and assist the children to print legibly, have them look at the alphabet across the top of any page. Invite them to print their favourite five letters. Have them search through the dictionary, select, and print five interesting words they found.

# Word Hunt

To connect words with their meanings and to use some basic conventions of formal texts (e.g., page numbers), have the children turn to a specific page which you identify initially by letter and number (e.g., an M page, page 66), then just by number. For example, you might choose a C page, page 24.

**Ask:** Can you put your finger on the picture that shows something sweet that you can eat? **(cake)** Can you put your finger on the word that means *speak loudly*? **(call)**

To reinforce the language grammar system (language syntax), have the children turn to the specific page where they will find the answers to your questions. For example, you might have them turn to page 25.

**Ask:** Can you finish this sentence? I went for a ride in our new _____ . **(car)**

Or you might choose page 23, and ask:

Can you find the missing word?
I like the taste of _____ on toast. **(butter)**

Some other possibilities are:

The dog is trying to jump over the _____ . **(fence)**
There is pink _____ on the birthday cake. **(icing)**

# Two Small Words

To help the children understand the meaning and composition of compound words, have them turn to a specific page. For example, you might have them turn to page 28.

**Say:** Which word means a place where people come together to learn? **(classroom)** Yes, the word is *classroom*. Why is it a compound word? **(made up of two small words — class and room)**

Or, on page 112:

Which word means *Saturday and Sunday*? **(weekend)** Yes, the word is *weekend*. What are the two small words that join together to make the word *weekend*? **(week and end)** When a long word is made up of two short words, what is the long word called? Yes, it's a compound word.

## Solve the Clue

To anchor word meanings, have the children turn to a specific page, and provide a clue about a particular word on the page. Then have them look over the page to find the answer to the clue. For example, you might have them turn to page 17.

**Say:** This is an animal that flies at night and that scares many people. **(bat)**

## Naming Words

To focus the children's understanding of nouns as people, places, and things, have them turn to a specific page. For example, you might have them turn to page 79:

**Ask:** What is the word that names a bird? **(pigeon)** What word names a thing that you put under your head when you're in bed? **(pillow)**

## Talk About It

To encourage the children to make use of words and pictures to create a message, have them turn to a specific page. Invite them to look at all the pictures and the boldface words and to choose one to talk about.

For example, a child might choose **stool** and talk about the stool that he has at home that he sits on when he watches television or looks at books. Another child might choose **boat** and talk about a boat ride she took on the lake at her friend's cottage.

## Reading Practice

To help the children read the sentences, have them turn to a specific page. For example, you might have them turn to page 26.

**Say:** What can Celia do with her baby sister? **(She can carry her.)**

**Then say:** Yes, Celia can carry her baby sister. What can Costa do with a ball? **(He can catch a ball.)** Yes. Costa can catch a ball.

## New Words

To help the children use the illustrations to figure out unknown words, have them turn to a specific page. Ask questions that focus on the picture content. For example, you might have them turn to page 26 for the word **ceiling**.

**Say:** Where is the man? **(at the top of a ladder)**
What is he doing? **(painting)** What is he painting? **(ceiling)**

Or you could ask:

What is he painting, the floor or the ceiling? Yes, he's painting the ceiling.

## Spelling

To help the children learn to spell some appropriate words, have them turn to a specific page. Invite them to respond to your questions by spelling the answers. For example, you might have them turn to page 26.

**Ask:** What is the name of the building where a king and a queen live? **(c-a-s-t-l-e)**
Yes. And what does c-a-s-t-l-e spell? Yes, that's right, it spells *castle*.

## New Words That Rhyme

To help the children use rhyming words to learn new words, have them turn to a specific page. For example, you might have them turn to page 26.

**Ask:** If this word says *cat*, how would I spell *bat*?

Or turn to page 35, and ask:

If this word says *dive*, how would I spell the place where a bee lives? **(h-i-v-e)**

## Personal Dictionary

To help the children develop a lasting love of words, establish a routine that every day they choose a favourite word from the dictionary and copy it legibly on the correct page in their personal dictionary.

# Aa  a b c d e f g h i j k l m

**accident**

I dropped the vase.
It was an accident.

**add**

Let's add another
block to the tower.

**afternoon**

In the afternoon we go
home from school.

**acrobat**

Look at the acrobat
at the circus.

**address**

My address is
42 Dove Place.

**again**

Amy jumps the rope
again and again.

**actor**

What is the actor
pretending to be?

**adult**

An adult is a man or
a woman.

**air**

Air is all around us
and above us.

n o p q r s t u v w x y z

# Aa

**airplane**

An airplane takes people up into the sky.

**alligator**

An alligator has a long tail.

**ambulance**

An ambulance takes people to a hospital.

**airport**

Airplanes come and go at the airport.

**alone**

Alex is alone. He is by himself.

**among**

There is one dog among all these cats.

**all**

Are all of these flowers yellow?

**alphabet**

Alissa knows the letters in the alphabet.

**anchor**

The anchor keeps the boat from moving far.

# Aa  a b c d e f g h i j k l m

**angry**

Adam is angry. Can you guess why?

**answer**

Amar knows the answer is 5.

**ape**

An ape is a kind of monkey with no tail.

**animal**

Cats and dogs and elephants are animals.

**ant**

An ant has six legs. Can you count them?

**apple**

An apple is a fruit that I like to eat.

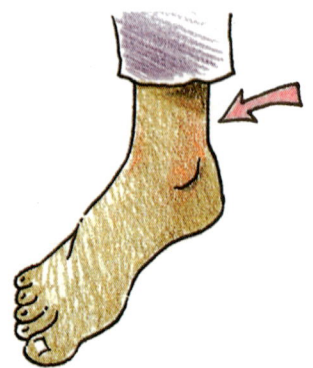

**ankle**

Your ankle joins your foot to your leg.

**apartment**

I live in the apartment on top of this building.

**arm**

You need strong arms to climb a rope.

# Aa

n o p q r s t u v w x y z

**ask**

I ask my mother if I can play outside.

**atlas**

An atlas is a book with maps inside.

**autumn**

It's autumn and the weather is colder.

**asleep**

It's night and the boy is asleep.

**audience**

The audience is listening to Anna sing.

**awake**

It's morning and the boy is awake.

**astronaut**

An astronaut travels through space.

**author**

A person who writes books is an author.

**axe**

This person is using an axe to chop wood.

# Bb

a b c d e f g h i j k l m

**baby**

The baby likes to play with his big sister.

**bad**

I can't eat this apple. It has gone bad.

**bag**

Becky is putting her books into a bag.

**bake**

Can you bake a cake in an oven?

**ball**

A ball is round and can roll down a hill.

**ballet**

Barbara wants to be a ballet dancer.

**balloon**

This blue balloon is full of air.

**banana**

A banana is a soft fruit with a thick skin.

**band**

Where can you hear a band play?

n o p q r s t u v w x y z   **Bb**

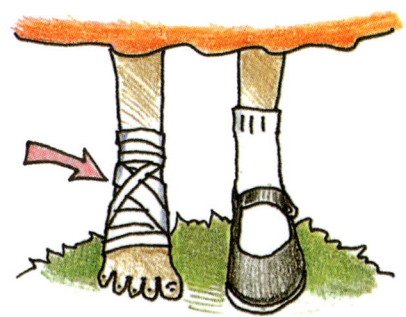

**bandage**

I have a bandage on my ankle.

**bark**

The dog likes to bark a lot.

**bat**

This is my dad's baseball bat.

**bang**

What made the door close with a bang?

**baseball**

My sister plays baseball with me.

**bat**

A bat is an animal that flies at night.

**barbecue**

Barney is cooking on the barbecue.

**basket**

The cat sleeps in a basket.

**bath**

Bonita is having a bath.

# Bb    a b c d e f g h i j k l m

**beach**

Brin is playing on the beach.

**bear**

A bear is a big, furry animal.

**bedroom**

The girl is playing in her bedroom.

**bead**

Can you put a bead on a string?

**beaver**

A beaver has a flat tail that helps it swim.

**bee**

A bee buzzes around flowers.

**bean**

We grow beans in our garden.

**bed**

Barry is in his bed. Is he asleep?

**beeper**

Mom gets messages on her beeper.

n o p q r s t u v w x y z  **Bb**

**before**

Beth finished her lunch before Ben.

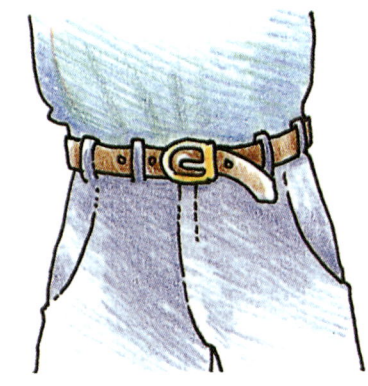

**belt**

My dad has a belt to keep his pants up.

**bike**

Another word for bicycle is bike.

**behind**

Bobby is behind the tree.

**bicycle**

I can ride my bicycle up a hill.

**bird**

A bird has wings, so it can fly.

**bell**

Brittany is pushing the bell.

**big**

An elephant has very big ears.

**birthday**

Today is my birthday. How old am I?

# Bb

a b c d e f g h i j k l m

**bite**

Bruce is taking a bite of his sandwich.

**boat**

My little sister plays with a toy boat.

**book**

How many books are in this picture?

**blanket**

Bart has a blanket to keep him warm.

**body**

Our cat's body has fur all over it.

**boot**

I am wearing my yellow boots.

**block**

Belinda is holding a red block.

**bone**

The dog is chewing on a big bone.

**borrow**

May I borrow your pen? I will give it back.

n o p q r s t u v w x y z **Bb**

**box**

Try to guess what is in the biggest box.

**bread**

Bread is made from flour.

**bridge**

This bridge goes over water.

**boy**

This is a boy. His name is Brendan.

**break**

If you drop a glass, it will break.

**bring**

Don't forget to bring your hat.

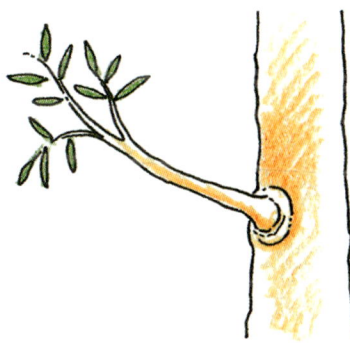

**branch**

A branch is a part of a tree.

**breakfast**

What am I eating for breakfast this morning?

**broccoli**

This vegetable looks like little trees. It's broccoli.

# Bb

a b c d e f g h i j k l m

**broom**

Barang uses a broom to sweep the floor.

**bubble**

I can make bubbles with soap and water.

**build**

I like to build big things with blocks.

**brother**

This is my big brother. He takes me to school.

**bucket**

You can carry water in a bucket.

**building**

Which of these buildings is a house?

**brush**

I brush my hair every morning.

**bug**

This bug can fly. Can you see its wings?

**bull**

There is a brown bull in the field.

n o p q r s t u v w x y z  **Bb**

**burn**

In the winter, I like to watch a fire burn.

**busy**

Brian is busy. He has work to do.

**button**

I am doing up a button on my coat.

**bus**

This bus can carry many people.

**butter**

Butter is made from cream.

**buy**

I have enough money to buy ice cream.

**bush**

This little bush has flowers growing on it.

**butterfly**

A butterfly is an insect with four big wings.

**buzz**

Can you hear the buzz of the bees?

# Cc

a b c d e f g h i j k l m

**cage**

We have a pet bird that lives in a cage.

**call**

My dad will call me when it's time to eat.

**camera**

I take photographs with my camera.

**cake**

I baked a cake in the oven.

**calm**

The water in the lake is very calm today.

**camp**

We like to camp outside in a tent.

**calendar**

A calendar shows all the months in a year.

**camel**

A camel has big flat feet.

**can**

Do you think Cara can reach the top shelf?

# Cc

n o p q r s t u v w x y z

**can**

Cory is drinking a can of lemonade.

**canoe**

Do you know how to paddle a canoe?

**card**

Cheri made a card for her friend's birthday.

**Canada**

We live in the country called Canada.

**cap**

I am wearing a blue cap.

**carpet**

My room has a blue carpet on the floor.

**candle**

This candle is too big for a birthday cake.

**car**

A car can go when the light is green.

**carrot**

A carrot grows under the ground.

# Cc  a b c d e f g h i j k l m

**carry**

Celia can carry her baby sister.

**catch**

Costa jumps up to catch the ball.

**cereal**

Charles is having cereal for breakfast.

**castle**

Would you like to live in a castle?

**cave**

Charlene has found a cave in the hill.

**chair**

Cathy is sitting in a big chair.

**cat**

Do you know what noise a cat makes?

**ceiling**

The man is painting the ceiling.

**chalk**

Our teacher writes with chalk.

n o p q r s t u v w x y z **Cc**

**cheek**

My mom kisses me on the cheek.

**chew**

We chew food with our teeth.

**children**

Children are girls or boys.

**cheese**

Cheese is made from milk.

**chicken**

A chicken lays eggs that we can eat.

**chocolate**

Chocolate is a sweet food.

**chest**

Your chest is above your stomach.

**child**

This child is a girl. Choose a name for her.

**choose**

Which piece of fruit shall I choose?

# Cc

a b c d e f g h i j k l m

**chop**

Dad is using a knife to chop vegetables.

**clap**

Clap your hands when you hear the music.

**clean**

The baby is clean after she has a bath.

**circus**

At the circus, there are clowns and acrobats.

**class**

How many children are in this class?

**climb**

It is dangerous to climb a ladder by yourself.

**city**

A city has a lot of tall buildings.

**classroom**

The children work in a big classroom.

**cloak**

The magician is wearing a black cloak.

n o p q r s t u v w x y z **Cc**

**clock**

What time is it on the clock?

**clothes**

I am wearing my new clothes.

**coat**

Cam has a blue coat for winter.

**close**

Close the door to keep the rain out.

**cloud**

I can see a big white cloud in the sky.

**coffee**

My mom drinks hot coffee.

**close**

My cat likes to sit close to me.

**clown**

A clown does tricks to make us laugh.

**cold**

It is a cold day and I have no gloves.

# Cc  a b c d e f g h i j k l m

**collar**

Cindy's new coat has a red collar.

**come**

Come here to me, little dog.

**cookie**

What kind of cookie do you like to eat?

**colour**

The colour of my hair is brown.

**computer**

I can type a message on a computer.

**cool**

The water feels cool on a hot day.

**comb**

Carla is doing her hair with a comb.

**cook**

Dad likes to cook. He is making soup.

**costume**

I have a pirate costume for the party.

n o p q r s t u v w x y z

# Cc

**cough**

Put your hand over your mouth when you cough.

**crab**

Do you know how a crab walks?

**crayon**

Crayons are good for drawing pictures.

**country**

Cali used to live in the country called Malaysia.

**crash**

The blocks fell over with a crash!

**cream**

There is cream in the middle of this cake.

**cow**

A cow is a farm animal that gives us milk.

**crawl**

The baby can crawl on his hands and knees.

**croak**

Can you hear the frog croak?

# Cc

a b c d e f g h i j k l m

**crocodile**

A crocodile has very sharp teeth!

**crown**

The queen has a gold crown on her head.

**cup**

This cup has hot coffee in it.

**cross**

I have made a big cross with my crayon.

**cry**

Sometimes I cry when I am very sad.

**cupboard**

We keep our toys in the cupboard.

**crow**

A crow is a big black bird.

**cucumber**

A cucumber can be put in a salad.

**cut**

What is Mom using to cut the apple?

n o p q r s t u v w x y z    **Dd**

**dad**

This is our dad. We are his children.

**dangerous**

It is dangerous to stand on the edge!

**daughter**

This is my mom and me. I'm her daughter.

**damp**

My hair is still damp. It is not dry yet.

**dark**

It is dark at night. We can't see the sun.

**day**

What day is it on this calendar?

**dance**

We like to dance to the music.

**date**

What is the date on this calendar?

**deep**

The water is deep. I can't touch the ground.

# Dd

a b c d e f g h i j k l m

**dentist**

A dentist helps us look after our teeth.

**dig**

Daisy can dig a deep hole.

**direction**

North, south, east, and west are directions.

**desk**

David is working at his desk.

**dinner**

My friend and I eat dinner together.

**dirty**

Don's hands are dirty. He has to wash them.

**diamond**

What a big diamond is in that ring!

**dinosaur**

Dinosaurs lived a long time ago.

**dish**

There is a lot of ice cream in the dish.

n o p q r s t u v w x y z **Dd**

**dive**

Danielle is going to dive into the pool.

**dog**

My dog likes to chew everything.

**donkey**

A donkey is smaller than a horse.

**divide**

Did we divide the jelly beans in half?

**doll**

A doll looks like a little person.

**door**

I will open the door and go outside.

**doctor**

A doctor can help us when we get sick.

**dolphin**

A dolphin has a pointed nose.

**down**

Diane is going down the slide.

# Dd

a b c d e f g h i j k l m

**dragon**

A dragon is not a real animal.

**dress**

What is the colour of my dress?

**drum**

Danny is playing the drums.

**draw**

Dean likes to draw pictures of fish.

**drink**

I am very thirsty. I need to have a drink.

**dry**

I am all dry now. I am not wet.

**dream**

Sometimes I dream that I can fly.

**drop**

My book was so heavy, I had to drop it.

**duck**

What sound does a duck make?

# Ee

n o p q r s t u v w x y z

**each**

Each of these glasses is empty.

**early**

It is very early in the morning.

**easy**

This puzzle is easy. Do you like puzzles?

**eagle**

An eagle is a big bird with a strong beak.

**earthworm**

An earthworm can help you to catch a fish.

**eat**

I am hungry. I am going to eat this apple.

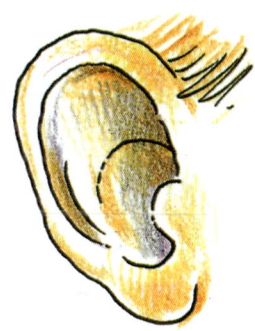

**ear**

I can hear with my ear.

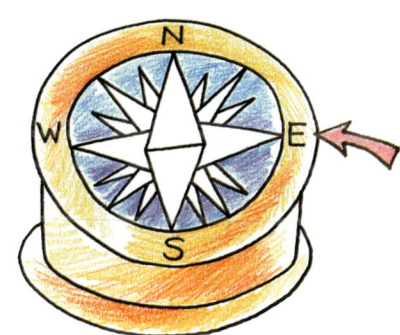

**east**

Which direction is east? Point to it.

**edge**

I am painting the edge of the box blue.

# Ee

a b c d e f g h i j k l m

**eel**

An eel is a long fish that looks like a snake.

**elephant**

What noise does an elephant make?

**empty**

This box is empty. There is nothing in it.

**egg**

Can you see the bird coming out of the egg?

**elevator**

An elevator takes you up or down.

**end**

This is the end of the story.

**elbow**

My elbow is the part of my arm that I bend.

**e-mail**

Mom is writing an e-mail to her friend.

**engine**

The engine of a car makes the car go.

n o p q r s t u v w x y z

# Ee

**enjoy**

Do you enjoy reading? Evan does.

**envelope**

Emil is putting the card into the envelope.

**evening**

The evening comes just before night.

**enough**

There is just enough milk to fill up my glass.

**equal**

The glasses have an equal amount of milk.

**every**

Every fish can swim. These are goldfish.

**entrance**

Here is the entrance. This is where we go in.

**eraser**

I fix mistakes with an eraser.

**everybody**

Everybody is sitting. Nobody is standing.

# Ee

a b c d e f g h i j k l m

**everyone**

Everyone is standing except the baby!

**excellent**

My teacher said my work was excellent.

**exit**

There is the exit. That is where we go out.

**everything**

Everything in the basket is a vegetable.

**exciting**

It is exciting to go on a plane.

**extra**

I have an extra hat. You can borrow it.

**example**

A piglet is an example of a baby animal.

**exercise**

My big sister dances for exercise.

**eye**

One eye and one eye makes two eyes.

n o p q r s t u v w x y z

# Ff

**face**

A face has a mouth, a nose, and eyes.

**fan**

I turned the fan on because I was hot.

**fast**

Franny can run very fast.

**fall**

Oops! I let the glass of milk fall.

**far**

I can throw a ball very far.

**fat**

Our cat eats a lot, so it is fat.

**family**

This is my family. This is my dad and my sister.

**farm**

What plants grow on this farm?

**father**

Another name for father is dad.

# Ff

a b c d e f g h i j k l m

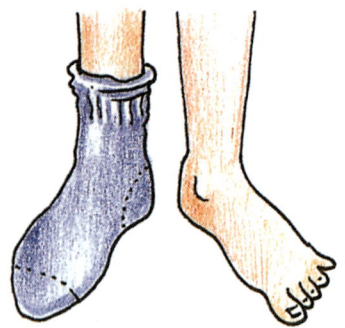

**feet**

I have two feet, but only one sock.

**find**

Frank is hiding. Fatima is trying to find him.

**fire**

Sometimes we make a fire to keep us warm.

**fence**

We have a fence so our dog can't get out.

**finger**

I am pressing the button with my finger.

**firefighter**

A firefighter puts out big fires.

**fill**

I can fill this pail with sand.

**finish**

I finish my milk quickly. Now it's all gone.

**fire truck**

Can you see the ladder on top of the fire truck?

n o p q r s t u v w x y z

# Ff

**first**

Fara came first in the race.

**flag**

This is Canada's flag. It is red and white.

**float**

Look at how the kites float in the air!

**fish**

A fish lives in water. Do you have a pet fish?

**flame**

Mom is blowing out the flame of the candle.

**flood**

The tap broke and now there is a flood.

**fix**

The woman is going to fix the broken chair.

**flat**

The top of a table is flat.

**floor**

The floor in the kitchen is black and white.

# Ff

a b c d e f g h i j k l m

**flour**

I use flour to make a cake.

**food**

The store sells all sorts of food.

**fork**

Francine is eating her food with a fork.

**flower**

Do you know the name of this flower?

**foot**

I have a sock on my foot.

**fountain**

Water is splashing in the fountain.

**fly**

Birds can fly from tree to tree.

**forest**

There are lots of trees in a forest.

**free**

The clown is giving out free balloons.

n o p q r s t u v w x y z

# Ff

**freezer**

I am putting the ice cream in the freezer.

**front**

The front of this house is painted blue.

**fun**

We have fun playing in the sand by the lake.

**friend**

My friend and I are playing together.

**fruit**

Can you name each fruit?

**funny**

The man looks funny with a red nose!

**frog**

This frog is jumping up high.

**full**

The glass is full of milk.

**fur**

The boy has a toy bear with soft fur.

# Gg

a b c d e f g h i j k l m

**game**

We are playing a game of tennis.

**garden**

What plants can you see in this garden?

**gerbil**

I have a gerbil for a pet.

**garage**

Mom puts our car in the garage.

**gas**

My big brother is filling his car with gas.

**get**

Dad is helping me get the ball out of the tree.

**garbage**

I put my broken toy in the garbage.

**gate**

Graham has left the gate open.

**giant**

Next to an ant, Gini looks like a giant!

n o p q r s t u v w x y z **Gg**

**gift**
Greg is wrapping a gift for the birthday party.

**give**
I give Mom flowers on her birthday.

**glass**
A window is made of glass.

**giraffe**
A giraffe has a very long neck.

**glad**
I am glad I have my umbrella today!

**glove**
Mom wears gloves to work in the garden.

**girl**
My sister Gloria is a girl.

**glass**
Can you guess what is in this glass?

**glue**
I use glue to stick the airplane together.

# Gg

a b c d e f g h i j k l m

**go**

We go to school on a bus like this.

**gold**

Necklaces and rings can be made of gold.

**goose**

A goose is bigger than a duck.

**goal**

Is this a goal? How do you know?

**good**

Grace is very good at running.

**grandfather**

My grandfather reads books with me.

**goat**

A baby goat is called a kid!

**goodbye**

We are waving goodbye to you.

**grandmother**

George's grandmother walks with him.

n o p q r s t u v w x y z **Gg**

**grape**

A grape is a small round fruit.

**great**

Look at the great size of the buildings!

**grow**

A kitten will grow to be a cat.

**grass**

My big brother is cutting the grass.

**ground**

Gio is lying on the ground having a rest.

**guess**

Can you guess which shoes are mine?

**grasshopper**

A grasshopper is an insect that jumps.

**group**

The kittens are all in a group.

**guitar**

I am learning to play the guitar.

# Hh   a b c d e f g h i j k l m

**hail**

Hail is little balls of ice that fall like snow.

**hamburger**

Hayden is having a hamburger for lunch.

**handle**

A handle lets you pick something up or open it.

**hair**

Helena has long black hair.

**hammer**

A hammer is used for hitting nails into wood.

**hang**

The shirts hang outside to dry.

**half**

We have used half of the box of eggs.

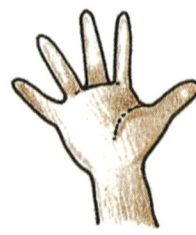

**hand**

This is my hand. Which hand is it?

**happy**

I am happy because it's my birthday!

n o p q r s t u v w x y z  **Hh**

**hard**

Hilary fell on the hard sidewalk!

**hay**

Hay is dry grass that some animals eat.

**hear**

I can hear the bird sing.

**hard**

Harry found it hard to jump over the puddle.

**head**

This is my head. Can you see my neck?

**heart**

This box is the shape of a heart.

**hat**

I wear a hat on a sunny day.

**healthy**

We are healthy. We are not sick.

**heat**

The heat from the fire keeps us warm.

# Hh   a b c d e f g h i j k l m

**heavy**

Hari could not lift the heavy box.

**hello**

Hugo sees his friend and says "Hello."

**here**

The treasure map told us to dig here.

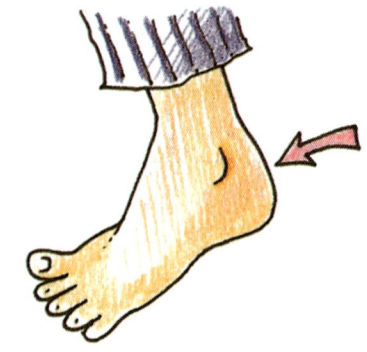

**heel**

The heel is the back part of your foot.

**helmet**

I wear a helmet when I am on my bike.

**high**

The switch is too high for the child to reach.

**helicopter**

Where is the helicopter going?

**help**

I like to help my father wash the car.

**hill**

We are going up the hill.

n o p q r s t u v w x y z **Hh**

**hiss**

The sound that snakes make is a hiss.

**hockey**

What else do I need when I play hockey?

**holiday**

We are going on a holiday!

**hit**

I must hit the ball. What game am I playing?

**hold**

My mother lets me hold my baby brother.

**hollow**

I can see my friend through the hollow tree.

**hive**

Bees live and work in a hive.

**hole**

The hole in the roof lets the rain in.

**home**

We are going home from school.

# Hh

a b c d e f g h i j k l m

**honey**

Honey is a sweet food made by bees.

**hoot**

I made a loud hoot on the trumpet.

**horse**

Did you ever sit on a horse?

**hood**

Hans has a hood on his jacket.

**horn**

Can you see one horn or two on the goat?

**hose**

We are washing the puppy with a hose.

**hook**

I am hanging my hat on the hook.

**horrible**

Hadley thinks that fish have a horrible smell.

**hospital**

Sick people can go to a hospital.

n o p q r s t u v w x y z

# Hh

**hot**

This chocolate is too hot to drink!

**house**

A house is a building that some people live in.

**hungry**

We are hungry. It's time to eat.

**hot dog**

Mmmm, I really like this hot dog! It's good!

**huge**

Henri is standing next to a huge rock.

**hurry**

We are in a hurry. We do not want to be late.

**hour**

The little hand tells you the hour.

**human**

Human is another word for person.

**hurt**

How did the girl hurt her arm?

# Ii

a b c d e f g h i j k l m

**ice**

Ice is frozen water.
I am skating on ice.

**icing**

There is pink icing on the birthday cake.

**inside**

The inside of the box is yellow.

**iceberg**

An iceberg floats in the ocean.

**ill**

Irina is too ill to go to school today.

**Internet**

I use the Internet to learn about dinosaurs.

**ice cream**

Isaac is eating chocolate ice cream.

**insect**

How many legs does an insect have?

**island**

An island is a bit of land with water all around.

n o p q r s t u v w x y z **Jj**

**jacket**

Jennifer is putting on her warm jacket.

**jeans**

Jody's jeans are too long for her.

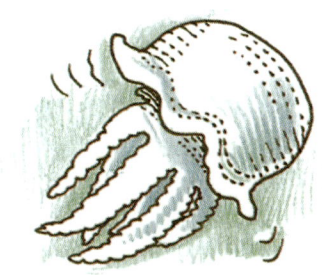

**jellyfish**

A jellyfish has a soft body.

**jam**

We are in a traffic jam. The cars can't go.

**jello**

Jello is a soft, sweet, shaky food.

**jet**

A jet is a very fast airplane.

**jar**

A jar is made of glass and has a lid.

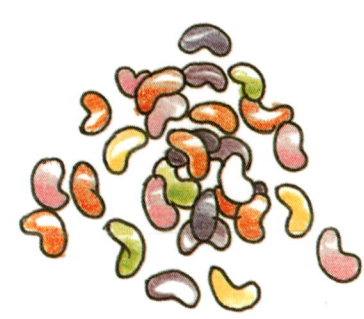

**jelly bean**

Jelly beans are candy. Are they soft like jello?

**jewel**

The woman is wearing a blue jewel.

# Jj

a b c d e f g h i **j** k l m

**jigsaw**

A jigsaw is a puzzle made of shapes.

**joke**

I am wearing clown's shoes as a joke.

**juice**

What kind of juice is this?

**job**

My mother is a farmer. That's her job.

**jug**

Juanita is pouring milk from the jug.

**jump**

Why can I jump so high?

**jog**

My brother is going for a slow jog.

**juggle**

The clown can juggle three balls at once.

**jungle**

Can you see the monkey in the jungle?

n o p q r s t u v w x y z    **Kk**

**kangaroo**

How does a kangaroo carry its baby?

**kettle**

The water in the kettle is very hot.

**kick**

I can kick the ball to you.

**kayak**

A kayak is like a canoe. They are boats.

**key**

Kim is opening the door with a key.

**kind**

Kar-Ling is very kind to her cat.

**ketchup**

The ketchup is in the red bottle.

**keyboard**

This is the keyboard of a computer.

**king**

The king is wearing a crown.

# Kk     a b c d e f g h i j k l m

**kiss**

My big sister gives me a kiss every morning.

**kitten**

A kitten is a baby cat. How many do you see?

**knife**

Kyle is spreading butter with a knife.

**kitchen**

A kitchen is a room where you cook food.

**knee**

Your knee is the part of your leg that bends.

**knock**

Knock to let someone know you are there.

**kite**

Kevin is flying his kite in the park.

**kneel**

Kiroko has to kneel to work in the garden.

**know**

I read this book and now I know more.

n o p q r s t u v w x y z   Ll

**ladder**

My father is climbing up the ladder.

**lamp**

Laura has turned on the lamp.

**large**

Do you know the name of this large bird?

**lake**

The ducks are swimming in the lake.

**land**

Our world is made up of land and water.

**last**

Leeann is eating the last cookie.

**lamb**

This animal is a lamb. It's a baby sheep.

**lap**

I am sitting on my grandfather's lap.

**laugh**

I always laugh when someone tickles me.

# Ll

a b c d e f g h i j k l m

**lawn**

My mother is cutting the lawn.

**leave**

At three o'clock the children leave school.

**lemon**

A lemon is a yellow fruit that tastes sour.

**leaf**

What kind of insect is on this leaf?

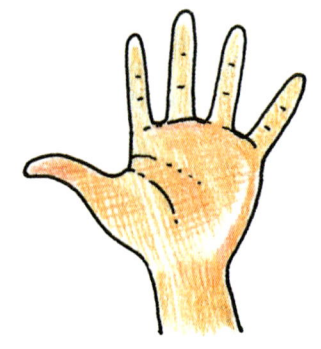

**left**

This is my left hand. Where is your left hand?

**leopard**

A leopard has yellow fur with black spots.

**learn**

What did this dog learn to do?

**leg**

Luke is standing on one leg.

**letter**

Lia is putting a letter in the mailbox.

n o p q r s t u v w x y z  **Ll**

**letter**

Which alphabet letter comes after B?

**lick**

I am going to lick the popsicle.

**lift**

Lucy has to lift her brother into his chair.

**lettuce**

There is lettuce in a lot of salads.

**lid**

This is a big lid. Guess what was in the jar.

**light**

The light is shining on the wall.

**library**

Latha is taking books back to the library.

**lie**

I lie down to have a rest.

**light**

This box is light. Maybe it's empty!

# Ll

a b c d e f g h i j k l m

**lightning**

You can see lightning during a storm.

**lips**

I kiss with my lips. Who do you kiss?

**live**

These people live in this house.

**line**

We are standing in line to buy a ticket.

**liquid**

Water is a liquid you can drink.

**lizard**

A lizard catches and eats insects.

**lion**

A lion is a big cat. What sound does it make?

**little**

I am very little next to my dad.

**lonely**

Lisa has nobody to play with. She is lonely.

n o p q r s t u v w x y z

**long**

Luis wears long pants, but Les wears shorts.

**lose**

I don't want to lose my toy, but I can't find it.

**love**

I love my new baby brother.

**look**

Look! Can you see an airplane in the sky?

**lot**

There are a lot of candles on the cake!

**low**

The apples are low so I can touch them.

**loose**

I untied my ribbon, so my hair is loose.

**loud**

What is making the loud bang?

**lunch**

We eat lunch in the middle of the day.

# Mm

a b c d e f g h i j k l m

**machine**

A machine helps us wash our clothes.

**man**

A man is a boy who has grown up.

**maple leaf**

There is a big maple leaf on Canada's flag.

**magnet**

What can you pick up with a magnet?

**many**

How many children do you see?

**mask**

Maria is wearing a funny mask.

**make**

Mia is going to make a train with her blocks.

**map**

There is a map of the world in our classroom.

**mat**

Miriam is sitting on a mat.

n o p q r s t u v w x y z

**meal**

We are sitting at the table having a meal.

**meet**

I am walking to meet my friends.

**metal**

Train tracks are made of metal.

**meat**

The meat is cooking on the barbecue.

**melon**

A melon is a large fruit with a very thick skin.

**middle**

What colour is the light in the middle?

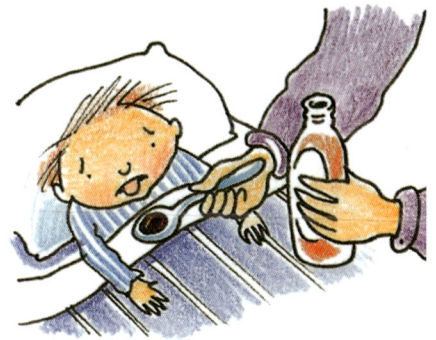

**medicine**

You take medicine when you are ill.

**message**

Marcel is giving Mary a message.

**milk**

I drink two glasses of milk every day.

# Mm  a b c d e f g h i j k l m

**minute**

Is a minute a long time or a short time?

**mitt**

Here is a mitt for each hand.

**monkey**

A monkey uses its tail to help it climb trees.

**mirror**

I am looking in the mirror. Who do I see?

**mom**

Another name for mother is mom.

**monster**

It's fun to dress up as a monster.

**mistake**

Martin has made a mistake with his socks.

**money**

You need money to buy things.

**moon**

At night you may see the moon in the sky.

n o p q r s t u v w x y z **Mm**

**moose**

A moose can eat plants that grow under water

**mountain**

A mountain is bigger than a hill.

**move**

Does this move quickly or slowly?

**morning**

I wake up early in the morning.

**mouse**

There's a mouse on the cheese!

**mud**

Maya has fallen in the mud!

**mother**

My mother is holding my hand.

**mouth**

I eat and drink and talk with my mouth.

**music**

I can play music on a guitar.

# Nn  a b c d e f g h i j k l m

**nail**

Niko is hitting a nail into a piece of wood.

**near**

Our house is near our neighbour's house.

**need**

I need a new pair of shoes.

**name**

My name is Noburu. What is your name?

**neat**

I have put my books in a neat pile.

**needle**

Mom is using a needle to fix my shirt.

**nap**

Nathan is having a nap on the floor.

**neck**

Your neck is below your head.

**neighbour**

Nina is my neighbour. Where does she live?

# Nn

n o p q r s t u v w x y z

**nest**

A nest is where birds have their home.

**newspaper**

A newspaper tells us what is going on.

**nightmare**

A nightmare is a bad dream.

**net**

This man is going to catch fish with a net.

**next**

The rabbits are next to each other.

**no**

You can shake your head to say no.

**new**

Nancy got a new bike for her birthday.

**night**

At night we go to bed to sleep.

**nobody**

There is nobody in the classroom.

# Nn  a b c d e f g h i j k l m

**noise**

Nicolas is making a lot of noise.

**north**

Which direction is north? Point to it.

**number**

Every shirt has a number on it.

**noodle**

Can I eat more than one noodle?

**nose**

I smell the flower with my nose.

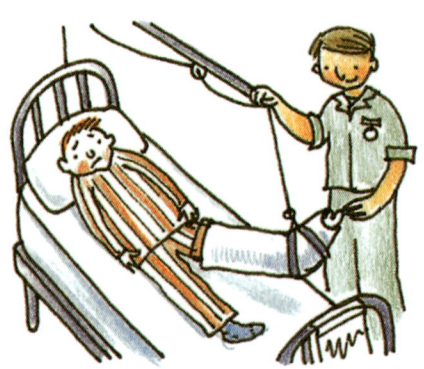

**nurse**

A nurse helps look after sick people.

**noon**

I eat lunch with my friend at noon.

**nothing**

There is nothing in the cupboard.

**nut**

A nut has a hard shell. Don't eat the shell!

n o p q r s t u v w x y z

# Oo

### oar
Each oar helps the boat to move.

### office
My mom works in an office.

### on
The toy is on the box. The box is on the table.

### ocean
An ocean is bigger than a lake.

### oil
Oil is a liquid that we use to cook food.

### once
Canada Day comes once every year.

### octopus
How many arms does an octopus have?

### old
I think my grandfather is very old.

### onion
An onion has a strong taste and smell.

# Oo    a b c d e f g h i j k l m

**open**

The gate is open. The cows will get out!

**orchestra**

Olivia plays a violin in the orchestra.

**oven**

Dad is getting the food out of the oven.

**orange**

An orange is a fruit with lots of juice.

**out**

What is Olga taking out of her bag?

**over**

Oona is jumping over the puddle.

**orchard**

An orchard is a large group of fruit trees.

**outside**

I am standing outside the circle.

**owl**

An owl is a bird that looks for food at night.

n o p q r s t u v w x y z

# Pp

**pack**

My little brother must pack his toys away.

**pail**

I can fill this pail with sand from the beach.

**pair**

Purna is wearing a pair of brown mitts.

**paddle**

You use a paddle to make a canoe move.

**paint**

What colour is the paint on the wall?

**palace**

A king and a queen live in this palace.

**page**

How many pictures are on this page?

**painting**

There are two paintings in my room.

**pants**

Phil is wearing new blue pants.

# Pp

a b c d e f g h i j k l m

**paper**

We use paper to write on.

**parents**

My mother and my father are my parents.

**part**

I have eaten part of this sandwich.

**parachute**

A parachute lets you float to the ground.

**park**

Peggy and Peri are playing in the park.

**party**

All my friends have come to my party.

**parcel**

Peter is carrying a parcel.

**park**

Lots of people park their cars here.

**path**

Let's walk along this path through the park.

n o p q r s t u v w x y z  **Pp**

**pea**

A pea is a small, round vegetable.

**pelican**

A pelican is a bird that eats fish.

**penguin**

A penguin is a bird but it can't fly.

**peach**

A peach is a fruit with a fuzzy skin.

**pen**

I am using a pen to write a letter.

**penny**

What is the picture on the back of a penny?

**pear**

A pear is a fruit that is like an apple.

**pencil**

Paul has a lot of coloured pencils.

**people**

How many people are in the picture?

# Pp  a b c d e f g h i j k l m

**person**

A person is someone like you or me.

**photograph**

This is a photograph of my class at school.

**picture**

I am drawing a picture of a tree.

**pet**

Pierre is feeding his pet cat. What is my pet?

**piano**

Pattie is learning to play the piano.

**pie**

Mom cuts the pie for us.

**phone**

Phone is another word for telephone.

**picnic**

My family is having a picnic at the lake.

**pig**

A pig is a farm animal with a flat nose.

n o p q r s t u v w x y z **Pp**

**pigeon**

A pigeon can fly, but it can walk around too.

**pilot**

A pilot flies planes up into the sky.

**pizza**

What kind of pizza do you like?

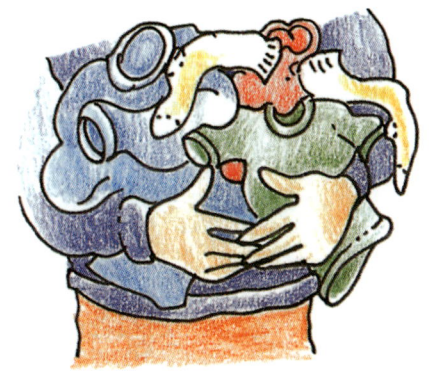

**pile**

Dad is carrying a pile of clothes.

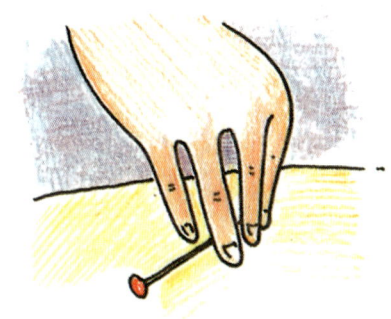

**pin**

I am picking up a pin from the floor.

**plane**

Another word for airplane is plane.

**pillow**

My pillow is soft under my head.

**pirate**

Each actor is dressed to look like a pirate.

**planet**

We all live on a planet called Earth.

# Pp   a b c d e f g h i j k l m

**plant**

A plant grows up from the ground.

**please**

May I have one of those, please?

**police officer**

A police officer can help people.

**plate**

This plate is round and flat.

**pocket**

One of my hands is in the pocket.

**pond**

Pava is feeding the ducks in the pond.

**play**

I play with my friends after school.

**point**

This knife has a very sharp point!

**pool**

Paco is diving into the pool.

n o p q r s t u v w x y z

# Pp

**popcorn**

Pilar is eating popcorn with her friend Pippa.

**pot**

The soup in the pot is getting warm.

**pretend**

Sometimes I pretend I'm a grown-up.

**popsicle**

A popsicle is sweet and cold.

**potato**

A potato is a vegetable that is white inside.

**pretty**

Look at the pretty lights on the tree.

**poster**

I put a poster on the wall in my room.

**present**

This is a present. Can you guess what it is?

**prize**

My drawing won first prize.

# Pp  a b c d e f g h i j k l m

**puddle**

Pablo is splashing in a puddle.

**puppet**

I can make the puppet dance.

**put**

I can put another block on top.

**pull**

I am trying to pull a lot of blocks.

**puppy**

A baby dog is called a puppy.

**puzzle**

Has Petra finished the puzzle?

**pumpkin**

A pumpkin is a large orange vegetable.

**push**

My brother is giving me a push.

**pyjamas**

Pat and her bear have the same pyjamas.

n o p q r s t u v w x y z  **Qq**

### quack
The sound that a duck makes is quack.

### queen
The queen has a crown on her head.

### quiet
I am being very quiet because they're asleep.

### quarter
How many quarters are in one dollar?

### question
My friend is asking me a question.

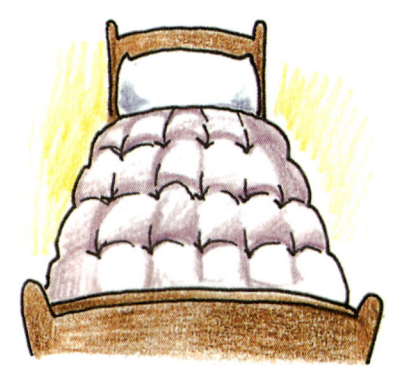

### quilt
The quilt on my bed is light and warm.

### quarter
Half of a half is a quarter.

### quick
Be quick or you will miss the bus!

### quiz
Our teacher lets us have a quiz every day.

# Rr  a b c d e f g h i j k l m

**rabbit**

A rabbit can eat a lot of vegetables.

**rain**

Rain is the water that falls from the sky.

**rat**

A rat is bigger than a mouse.

**raccoon**

A raccoon looks for food at night.

**rainbow**

When do you see a rainbow in the sky?

**rattlesnake**

What sound does a rattlesnake make?

**race**

I ran fast in the race and I was first.

**rake**

A rake helps you pick up leaves.

**read**

I like to read. What story do you like best?

n o p q r s t u v w x y z

# Rr

**ready**

Ruth is getting ready for school.

**rest**

My puppy is having a rest.

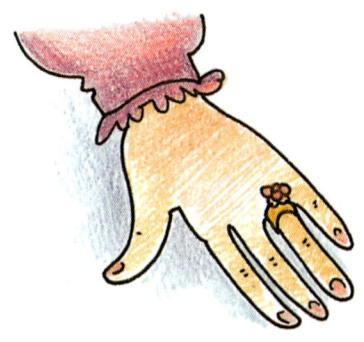

**ring**

The ring is on a woman's finger.

**refrigerator**

A refrigerator keeps food cold.

**ride**

I am learning to ride my new bike.

**river**

It would be dangerous to swim in this river!

**reindeer**

Many reindeer live in the north of Canada.

**right**

I point with one finger of my right hand.

**road**

How many cars are on this road?

85

# Rr    a b c d e f g h i j k l m

**roar**

A roar is the sound a lion makes.

**rocket**

A rocket moves very fast.

**room**

There are two chairs and a bed in my room.

**robot**

A robot is a machine that helps us do work.

**roll**

I can roll the ball to my friend.

**rooster**

What noise does a rooster make?

**rock**

The man is going up the side of the rock.

**roof**

The roof of this house is red.

**root**

The root of a plant is under the ground.

n o p q r s t u v w x y z

# Rr

**rope**

Ralph is swinging on the rope.

**row**

These trees are all in rows.

**rug**

I am wrapped in the rug on the floor.

**rose**

A rose is a flower with a good smell.

**row**

You need oars to row a boat.

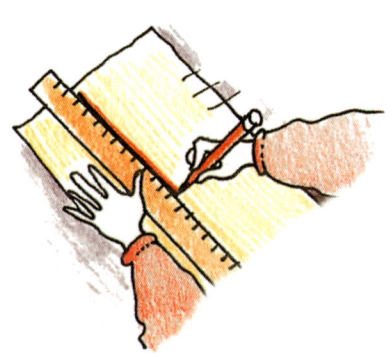

**ruler**

I am drawing a line with a ruler.

**round**

Which of these shapes is round?

**rub**

I rub my hands together to keep warm.

**run**

I like to run with my dog.

# Ss

a b c d e f g h i j k l m

**sack**

The man is carrying a sack on his back.

**salt**

Is Susie putting too much salt on her food?

**saucer**

The saucer goes under the cup.

**sad**

Simon is sad. He has nobody to play with.

**sand**

I like to play in the sand on a beach.

**saw**

A saw is very sharp. It can cut wood.

**salad**

This salad has lots of vegetables.

**sandwich**

I am eating a big sandwich for lunch.

**scare**

Sally jumped up to scare her brother.

n o p q r s t u v w x y z **Ss**

**school**

A school is where children go to learn.

**scream**

We are going so fast that we want to scream!

**seatbelt**

Always wear a seatbelt in a car.

**scissors**

Scissors are good for cutting out shapes.

**sea**

Many kinds of fish live in the sea.

**second**

The boy in green is second in the line.

**scratch**

Steve has a scratch on his arm.

**seagull**

Is Stephanie feeding every seagull?

**see**

What can you see in this picture?

# Ss   a b c d e f g h i j k l m

**seed**

A seed becomes a plant.

**shallow**

The water is shallow. It is a bit over my feet.

**shark**

A shark is a very big fish.

**send**

I want to send a present to my friend.

**shampoo**

Sean is having his hair washed with shampoo.

**sharp**

This axe has a very sharp edge.

**shake**

I can shake the rug to clean it.

**shape**

Can you name each shape?

**sheep**

A sheep is an animal with a coat of wool.

n o p q r s t u v w x y z **Ss**

**shelf**

Can Sarah reach the shelf?

**shirt**

Salim is wearing a yellow shirt.

**short**

My skirt is short but my sister's is long.

**shell**

There are lots of shells on this beach.

**shiver**

I am so cold I am starting to shiver.

**shorts**

I'm wearing a pair of blue shorts.

**ship**

A ship is a big boat. It goes on the ocean.

**shoe**

I have a new pair of brown shoes.

**shoulder**

Your shoulder is below your neck.

# Ss     a b c d e f g h i j k l m

**shout**

I have to shout so my friend can hear me.

**sick**

Samir is sick. He is not feeling well.

**silly**

This man looks silly with his face painted.

**show**

Sylvia opened the bag to show me her kitten.

**side**

This is the side of a ___ ?

**silver**

Sulu likes to touch her silver necklace.

**shower**

I am washing myself in the shower.

**sign**

Do you know what this sign says?

**sing**

I like to sing while Mom plays the piano.

n o p q r s t u v w x y z

# Ss

**sink**

This toy boat is starting to sink!

**sit**

Sheila is going to sit on the chair.

**skirt**

Mom is wearing a green skirt.

**sink**

The dirty dishes are in the sink.

**skate**

My big sister has skates like these.

**sky**

The sky is very blue in this picture.

**sister**

Sue is Sam's sister. They have the same dad.

**skin**

This is a banana skin. What colour is it?

**sleep**

Saito has gone to sleep.

# Ss   a b c d e f g h i j k l m

**sleeve**

Dad has rolled up each sleeve.

**slow**

This is a turtle. It is a slow animal.

**smile**

I smile when I am happy.

**slide**

Scott likes to slide. He is going fast.

**small**

Ants are very small. How many are there?

**snack**

A snack is a small meal that I can eat quickly.

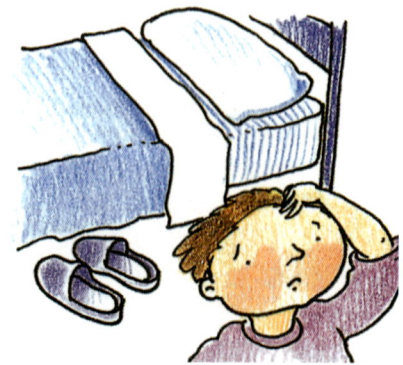

**slipper**

I cannot see my slippers. Can you?

**smell**

I like the smell of flowers.

**snake**

A snake is a long animal with a dry skin.

n o p q r s t u v w x y z **Ss**

**sneeze**

Shannon uses a tissue to sneeze.

**snorkel**

I have a snorkel so I can swim underwater.

**sock**

Soula cannot find her other sock.

**sniff**

Dogs like to sniff shoes!

**snow**

Simone is playing in the snow.

**soft**

This sand is very soft. Where are my feet?

**snore**

I can hear my dad snore when he sleeps.

**soap**

I am washing my hands with soap.

**soil**

Can you see a plant growing in the soil?

# Ss

a b c d e f g h i j k l m

**son**

My father is my grandfather's son.

**soup**

We are going to have alphabet soup!

**spade**

You can dig a hole with a spade.

**song**

The children are singing a song.

**sour**

Lemons have a sour taste.

**spaghetti**

I am twisting spaghetti around my fork.

**sound**

What sound can I hear?

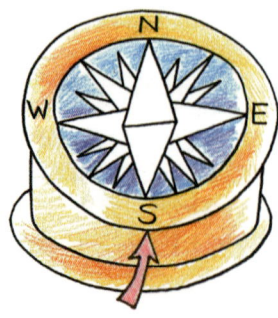

**south**

Which direction is south? Point to it.

**speak**

My baby brother is learning to speak.

n o p q r s t u v w x y z  **Ss**

**spell**

I can spell towel.
t – o – w – e – l

**spoon**

I use a spoon to eat cereal.

**stack**

Shane is putting his books in a stack.

**spider**

How many legs does a spider have?

**sport**

A sport can be a game or exercise.

**stairs**

Selma is walking up the stairs to her room.

**splash**

Sunita is making a splash in the water.

**spring**

After winter is spring. Flowers start to grow.

**stamp**

A letter needs a stamp.

# Ss

a b c d e f g h i j k l m

**stand**

Bears stand if they want to scare you.

**statue**

There is a statue of a horse in the park.

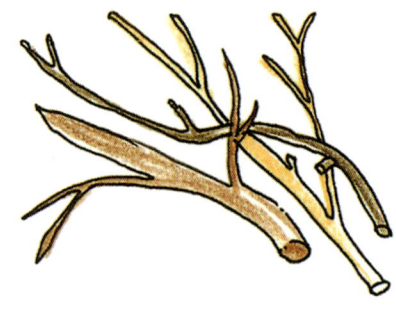

**stick**

A stick is a thin piece of wood.

**star**

Every star is in the sky.

**stem**

The stem grows from the root of a plant.

**stick**

What will I use to stick pictures in a book?

**start**

The race is going to start.

**step**

This baby is learning to take a step.

**sticker**

My bag is covered with stickers!

n o p q r s t u v w x y z **Ss**

**sting**

Some insects can sting and hurt you.

**stone**

Each stone is near the pond.

**store**

What can you buy in this store?

**stir**

Dad is using a spoon to stir the soup.

**stool**

A stool is a seat with no back.

**storm**

It is good to be inside when there is a storm.

**stomach**

Your stomach is in the middle of your body.

**stop**

Cars must stop when the traffic light is red.

**story**

I am reading a story in my book.

# Ss  a b c d e f g h i j k l m

### stove
When you turn on a stove, it gets very hot.

### streetcar
Like a train, a streetcar moves on tracks.

### study
My sister has to study for a test.

### strawberry
A strawberry is a fruit that is red and sweet.

### string
My kitten likes to play with a ball of string.

### suck
I like to suck my orange juice slowly.

### street
I live on Wood Street. Where do you live?

### strong
My dad is strong. He can lift heavy things.

### sugar
Mom puts sugar in coffee to make it sweet.

n o p q r s t u v w x y z **Ss**

**summer**

Summer is the hottest time of the year.

**surprise**

A surprise can make you jump!

**swim**

Safar likes to swim in the pool.

**sun**

The sun gives us heat and light.

**swan**

A swan is a big bird with a long neck.

**swing**

I love to swing high in the air.

**sunscreen**

Sunscreen stops your skin from burning.

**sweet**

Something is sweet if it tastes like sugar.

**switch**

Will Sheena turn the switch on or off?

# Tt

a b c d e f g h i j k l m

**table**

This is the kitchen table in our house.

**talk**

I like to talk with my friend Tony.

**taxi**

This taxi took us to the airport.

**tail**

When a dog is happy it waves its tail.

**tap**

I am turning on the tap to get some water.

**tea**

My grandmother likes to drink tea.

**take**

Terri is trying to take off her boots.

**taste**

Theo is having a taste to see if he likes it.

**team**

My sister plays on this basketball team.

n o p q r s t u v w x y z  **Tt**

**telephone**

I call my friend on the telephone.

**temperature**

The temperature tells you how warm it is.

**thanks**

I am saying thanks to my grandmother.

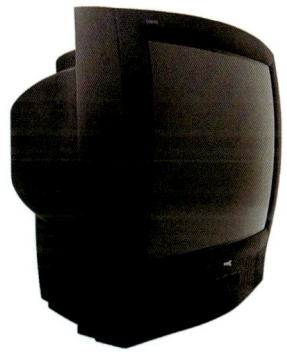

**television**

Another name for a television is a TV.

**tennis**

We are playing a game of tennis.

**that**

That is my bicycle. Do you have a bicycle?

**tell**

Tamar is going to tell a story to the class.

**tent**

When we go camping, we sleep in a tent.

**thick**

I have made a thick black line on the paper.

# Tt  a b c d e f g h i j k l m

**thin**

I have made a thin black line on the paper.

**this**

I enjoyed reading this book.

**ticket**

You need a ticket to get on a plane.

**think**

Toby has to think hard to get the answer.

**throw**

Tina can throw the ball a long way.

**tie**

I tie my dog up when I go into a store.

**thirsty**

The bottle is empty and I am still thirsty!

**thunder**

Thunder is the loud noise after lightning.

**tiger**

What colour are the stripes on a tiger?

n o p q r s t u v w x y z **Tt**

**time**

The time is five minutes before six.

**tissue**

The tissue is soft on my nose.

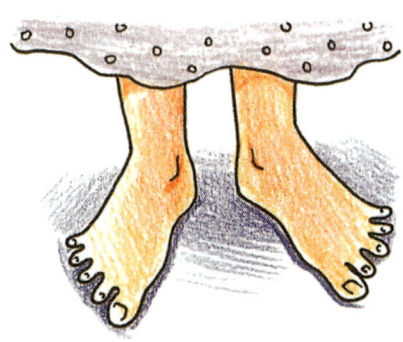

**toe**

I have a big toe on each foot.

**tiny**

From up here, the cars look tiny.

**toast**

The toast is ready to eat.

**together**

Tara and her mom are walking together.

**tire**

What is wrong with this tire?

**today**

Today is the first of May. It's my birthday.

**tomato**

This tomato is going to be made into ketchup.

# Tt

a b c d e f g h i j k l m

**tomorrow**

Tom's clothes are ready for tomorrow.

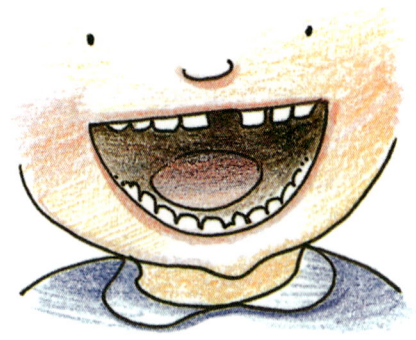

**tooth**

I have lost a tooth! Will I grow another one?

**towel**

Tiffany is drying her hair with a towel.

**tongue**

Your tongue helps you to eat and to speak.

**top**

It's a long way up to the top of a ladder.

**town**

A town is not as big as a city.

**tool**

Which tool do you use to cut wood?

**touch**

I like to touch my cat's fur. It feels very soft.

**toy**

Ted is playing with his new toy.

n o p q r s t u v w x y z  **Tt**

**track**

The train is moving along the track.

**train**

The train is coming into the station.

**trick**

I am teaching my dog a trick.

**tractor**

A tractor is used for pulling heavy things.

**treasure**

This box is full of gold and other treasure.

**truck**

This truck is carrying a lot of wood.

**traffic**

This road is full of traffic.

**tree**

Can you see the roots of the tree?

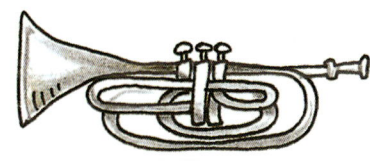

**trumpet**

You play a trumpet by blowing into it.

# Tt

a b c d e f g h i j k l m

**try**

My brother walks fast and I try to keep up.

**tuque**

My tuque keeps my head warm.

**twin**

My sister is my twin. We are six years old.

**T-shirt**

Tabitha is wearing an orange T-shirt.

**turn**

The wheels of a car turn very quickly.

**twist**

We twist a wet towel to get the water out.

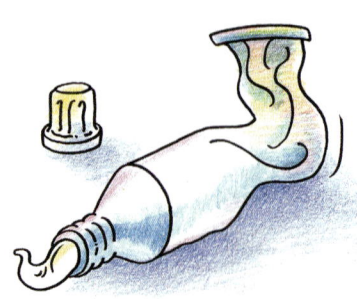

**tube**

Guess what is inside this tube.

**turtle**

The body of a turtle is inside a hard shell.

**type**

Dad is going to type a letter on the computer.

# Uu

n o p q r s t u v w x y z

**ugly**

My brother is wearing an ugly mask.

**underwear**

I am not dressed. I am still in my underwear.

**up**

We are walking up a big hill.

**umbrella**

An umbrella keeps you dry in the rain.

**uniform**

We are wearing our team uniform.

**upside down**

Look at me! I'm upside down!

**under**

I am hiding under the table.

**universe**

The universe has many, many stars.

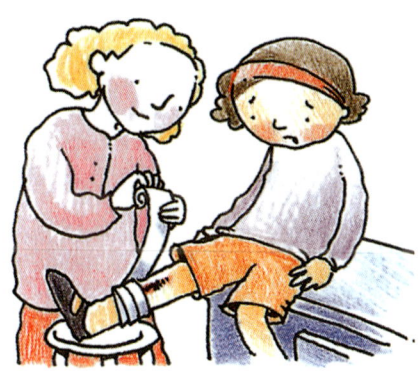

**use**

Mom had to use a bandage on my leg.

# Vv

a b c d e f g h i j k l m

**vacuum cleaner**

A vacuum cleaner sucks up dirt.

**vet**

A vet is a doctor for animals.

**visit**

We are going to visit our friends.

**vase**

This vase has yellow and red flowers in it.

**video**

Vicky is watching a video.

**voice**

My big brother has a very loud voice.

**vegetable**

Which vegetable do you like best?

**violin**

I play the violin every day.

**volcano**

Hot rocks from the volcano are flying up!

n o p q r s t u v w x y z **Ww**

**wait**

We have to wait for the bus.

**warm**

I am warm because I am near the heater.

**watch**

I like to watch the kites fly.

**walk**

William is going for a walk beside the lake.

**wash**

Wash your hands before you eat.

**watch**

I know the time when I wear my watch.

**wall**

Wanda is throwing a ball against the wall.

**waste**

We waste a lot of food.

**water**

Is the water in the glass hot or cold?

# Ww    a b c d e f g h i j k l m

**watermelon**

A watermelon is green outside and pink inside.

**web**

The spider made a web between the trees.

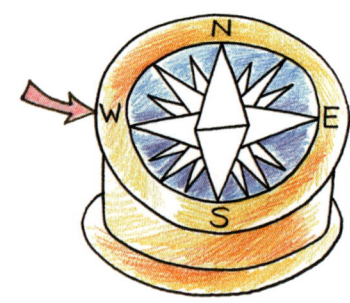

**west**

Which direction is west? Point to it.

**wave**

Wayne can wave goodbye to his friends.

**week**

A week is seven days long.

**wet**

Wilma got wet in the rain.

**wave**

The wave is splashing on the beach.

**weekend**

The weekend is Saturday and Sunday.

**whale**

A whale needs air to live. It is not a fish.

n o p q r s t u v w x y z  **Ww**

**what**

What time is it on this clock?

**where**

Where did I put my hat?

**whisper**

A whisper is a very quiet way of talking.

**wheel**

One wheel is bigger than the others.

**which**

Which of these cars is red? Point to it.

**who**

Who is the smallest child in this picture?

**when**

When is my mom coming to pick me up?

**while**

Ward sits on the swing while I give it a push.

**whole**

I want to eat the whole pizza!

# Ww

a b c d e f g h i j k l m

**why**

The woman is angry with the boy. Why?

**wing**

Birds flap each wing to fly.

**with**

I am walking to school with Wendy.

**wind**

The wind blew my hat away.

**winter**

The coldest time of the year is winter.

**without**

I am walking to school without Wendy.

**window**

I can see my friend through the window.

**wish**

I wish I had a horse. What do you wish for?

**woman**

A woman is a girl who has grown up.

n o p q r s t u v w x y z  **Ww**

**wood**

The wood is ready for the fire.

**work**

I like to work in the garden with my dad.

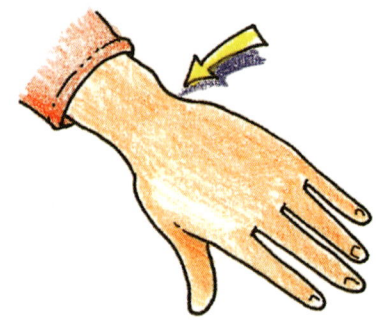

**wrist**

Your wrist joins your hand to your arm.

**wool**

Sheep grow wool that we use to make clothes.

**world**

This is our world. Can you point to Canada?

**write**

My sister can write all the alphabet letters.

**word**

Did you learn a new word today?

**worm**

There's a worm in this apple!

**wrong**

The answer 5 is wrong. The answer is 4.

# XYZ  a b c d e f g h i j k l m

**X ray**

This X ray is a picture of a person's bones.

**yak**

A yak lives in cold countries.

**year**

How many days are there in one year?

**xylophone**

I have learned to play the xylophone!

**yard**

My friend's front yard is next to mine.

**yell**

Yuri is far away, so Yolanda has to yell.

**yacht**

A yacht is a boat that doesn't need an engine.

**yawn**

Ya-Kee is so tired, he has started to yawn.

**yes**

You can nod your head to say yes.

n o p q r s t u v w x y z

# xyz

**yesterday**

The day before today was yesterday.

**yo-yo**

I am playing with my yo-yo.

**zigzag**

This skirt has a zigzag around it.

**yolk**

The yolk is the yellow part of the egg.

**zebra**

A zebra looks like a horse with stripes.

**zipper**

The zipper on Zack's jacket is stuck.

**young**

Do you know what a young horse is called?

**zero**

5, 4, 3, 2, 1, zero! The rocket took off!

**zoo**

Zoe likes the giraffes at the zoo.

# Words We Use a Lot

## Aa
about
above
after
against
almost
along
also
always
am
amount
and
another
any
are
around
as
at
ate
away

## Bb
back
be
because
been
began
begin
being
below
best
better
between
both
but
by

## Cc
carefully
clear

## Dd
do
doesn't
done
don't

## Ee
enter
even
ever
exactly
expect

## Ff
favourite
few
fine
for
force
form
found
fraction
from

# Words We Use a Lot

**Gg**
- gave
- going
- gone
- got

**Hh**
- had
- has
- have
- he
- her
- hers
- him
- his
- how

**Ii**
- I'll
- icicle
- idea
- if
- important
- in
- into
- is
- it, it's, its
- itself

**Jj**
- join
- judge
- jumbo
- just

**Kk**
- karate
- keen
- keep

**Ll**
- later
- let
- life
- like
- list
- lock
- log
- lost

**Mm**
- made
- mail
- mark
- may
- me
- men
- might
- mine
- miss
- more
- most
- much
- must
- my

# Words We Use a Lot

## Nn
- never
- nor
- not
- note
- now

## Oo
- of
- off
- often
- oh
- only
- or
- other
- our
- own

## Pp
- passed
- past
- period
- piece
- place

## Qq
- quit
- quite

## Rr
- radio
- rail
- ramp
- ran
- rare
- reach
- real
- really
- remember
- rich

## Ss
- said
- say
- seem
- sentence
- set
- shall
- she
- since
- so
- some
- somebody
- someone
- something
- sometimes
- soon
- sort
- space
- stay
- still
- student
- such

# Words We Use a Lot

**Tt**
tall
teacher
than
their
theirs
them
they
thing
thought
through
to, too
told
took
toward
travel
trip
true

**Uu**
unless
until
us
usually

**Vv**
vacant
van
very
view
village
vowel

**Ww**
want
was
way
we
weather
well
went
were
wide
wild
will
worker
would

**Xx**
x's and o's

**Yy**
yet
you
your
you're
yourself

**Zz**
zap
zone

# Colours

# Numbers and Coins

| | |
|---|---|
| 1 | one |
| 2 | two |
| 3 | three |
| 4 | four |
| 5 | five |
| 6 | six |
| 7 | seven |
| 8 | eight |
| 9 | nine |
| 10 | ten |
| 100 | one hundred |
| 1000 | one thousand |
| 1 000 000 | one million |

 cent

 nickel

 dime

 quarter

 loonie

 toonie

# Shapes

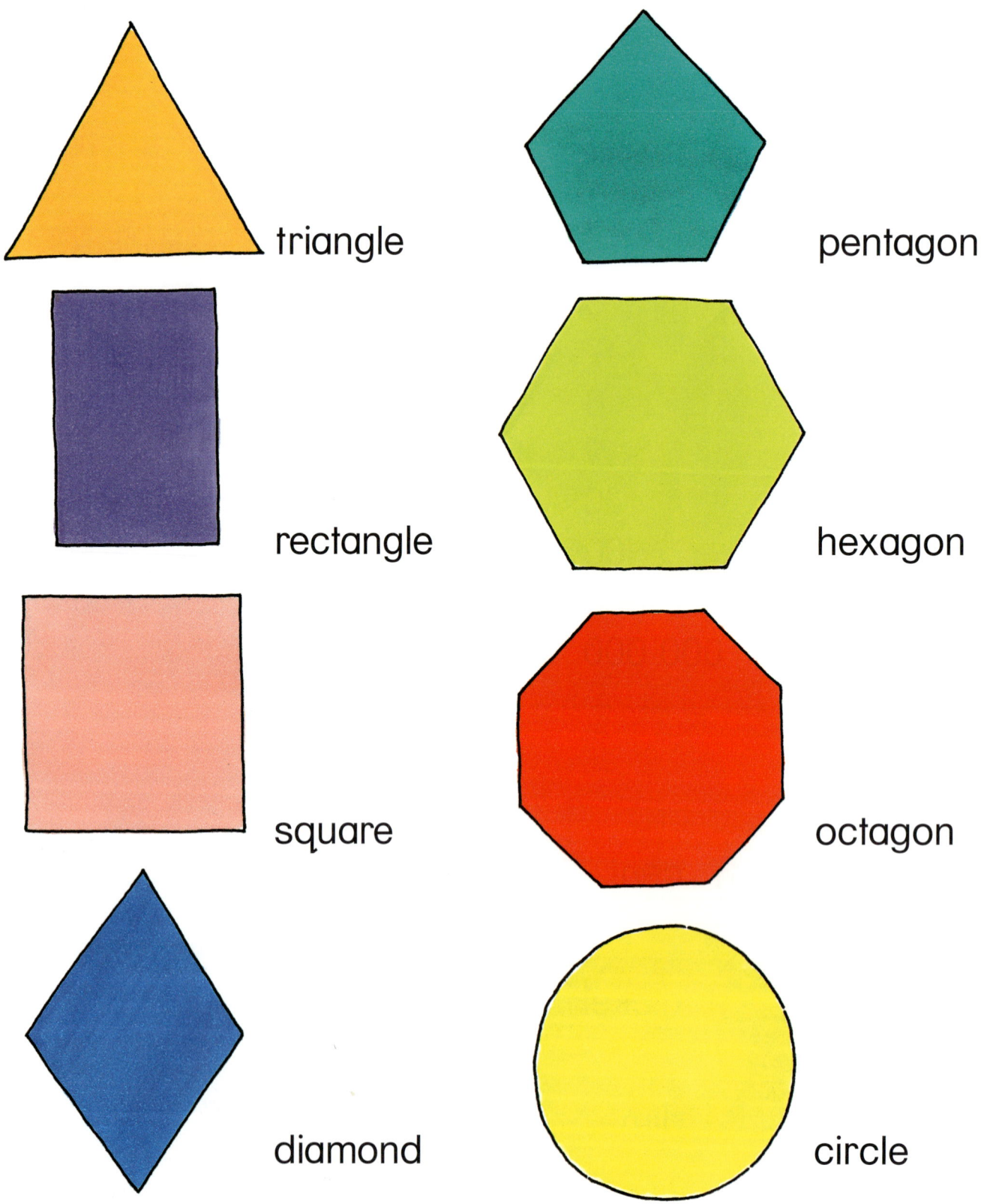

# Solids

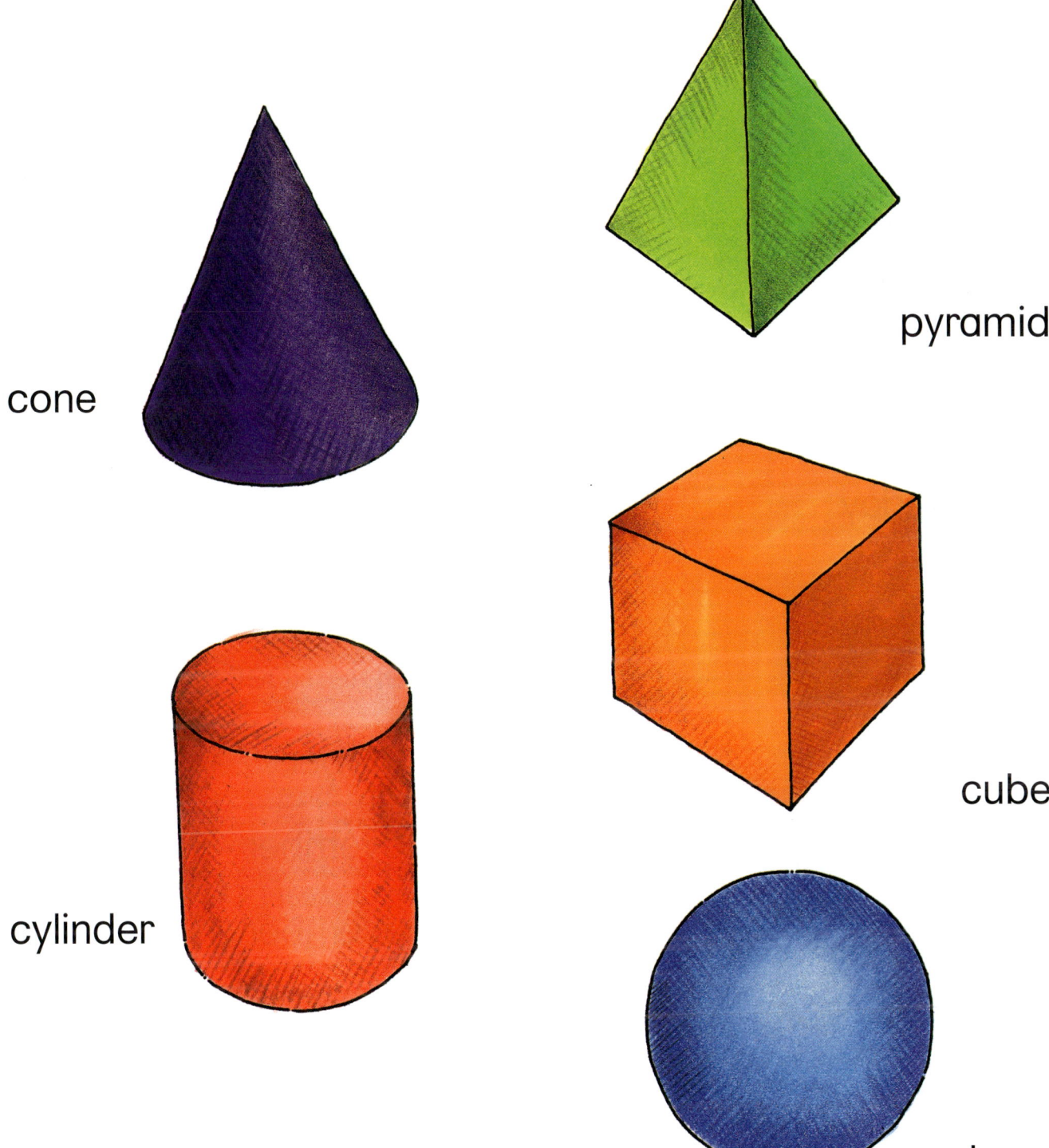

125

# Days, Months, and Seasons

**Days**

Monday

Tuesday

Wednesday

Thursday

Friday

Saturday

Sunday

**Months**

January

February

March

April

May

June

July

August

September

October

November

December

**Seasons**

Spring

Summer

Fall or Autumn

Winter

# Our Solar System

# Map of Canada